Adaptive

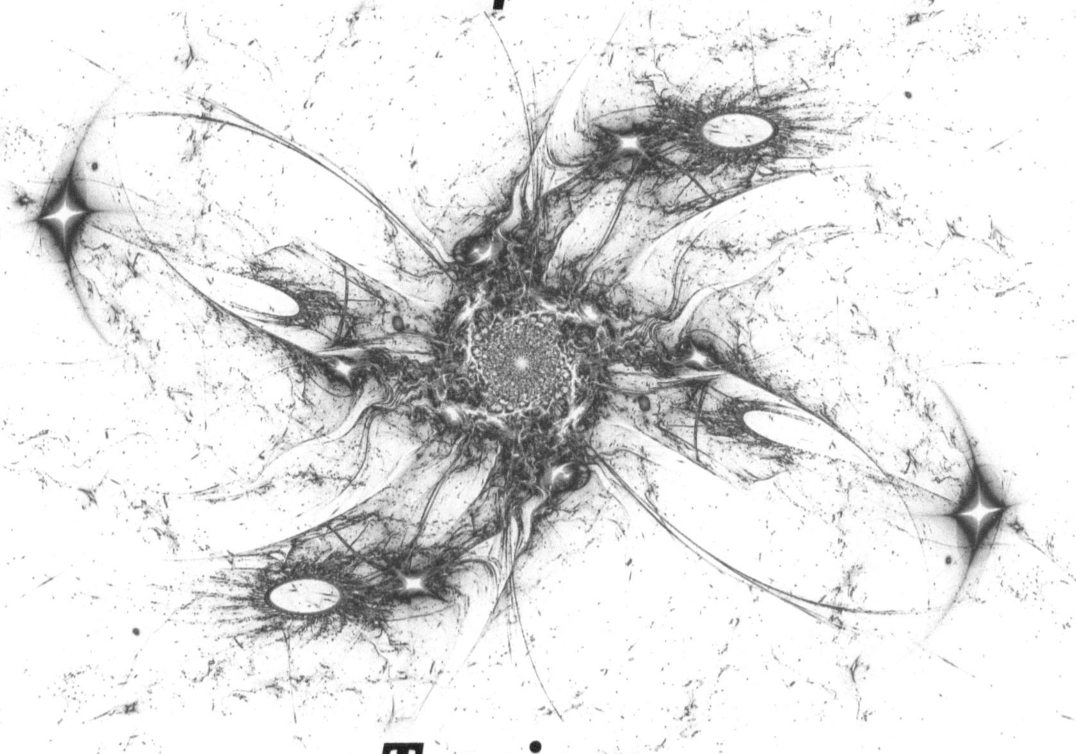

Tensions

Ron Rubin

Design and layout by
Inkfall Studios
New Haven, Vermont

Dedication

To Lisa, Micah, Jesse, and my dearest friends who inspire my writing, support every word, and encourage me to become who I am.

Contents

Remarks

When I think about the feeling of tension I often conjure up the kinds I deplore. The kinds I try to prevent, deny, avoid, or positively cope with as best I can. These are the kinds of tensions that accompany lingering discord and conflicts I have with family members; having a "to do" list that outstrips the time I need to attend to the items listed; working a task where my and/or other's expectations and demands surpass the support given to accomplish its fulfillment; or when I'm feeling angst concerning the condition of our planet and humanity. The tensions from which I seek safe haven might combine all the above along with a heap of others. These are the kinds of tensions I experience when I feel overwhelmed and powerless. They are maladaptive.

My responses to maladaptive types of tension determine how they affect me physically, mentally, emotionally and spiritually. They offer me the opportunity to ask questions about my purpose; to look more closely at how I address the various kinds of dis-ease I suffer; to take stock of my resources and how I use them; to adopt a "new order"; and to live that new order to the full extent of my capabilities. My responses can turn maladaptive tensions into adaptive tensions. When this occurs frequently over time, I'm less vulnerable to maladaptive tensions. My physical, mental, emotional and spiritual immune systems are better equipped, and I feel overwhelmed and powerless less often.

Balancing the dynamic interplay between the maladaptive and adaptive tensions in my life isn't easy to achieve. Nor is exerting the effort and developing the necessary skills a simple matter. The intended affects and the results of my efforts, although important and desired, aren't the measure of success. In fact, as much as my ego revels in accomplishing positive outcomes, success is irrelevant. Making the effort is what really concerns me. I believe by making the effort to balance the types of tensions I experience that I contribute, even if only in the smallest of ways, to my welfare, the welfare of others, and the welfare of our planet. If my belief derives from an over-extended ego, then I've fooled myself. Even so, what I believe is real in its effects.

I also lean towards the notion that efforts devoted to maintaining balance between maladaptive and adaptive tensions can be exerted collectively by all "species" of community. Here again I subscribe to the idea that making the effort in and of itself contributes to realizing positive effects and contributes to an enhanced quality of health for those communities that collectively extend the effort.

Adaptive Tensions *is a book of poetry that embraces and expresses the above ideas. Most of the poems were written over the past seven years, some of them quite a while ago. They chronicle my balancing act regarding maladaptive and adaptive tensions...within myself, with others, and with all that surrounds me near and far.*

Ron
November 2015

Adaptive Tensions

1. The Tension

the tension sometimes overwhelms
the tension is the struggle with hypocrisy
the arm-wrestling with ego and arrogance
the tension is the abuse of power
the tension is disillusionment
it is dejection
rejection
despair
cynicism
it is the feeling of impossibility
it is hopelessness
it is inside and outside myself

2. Adaptive

adaptive is the power of renewal
adaptive is the courage of honesty
it is the resilience of mountains
the balancing of our own and other's needs
adaptive is knowing the transcendent
acting with strength and integrity
it is uplifting
welcoming
heartening
confident
it is what feels within reach
it is optimism
it is inside and outside myself

Endangered

What I've learned in my life tells me that punishing, shaming, and/or humiliating a person, group, or nation doesn't lead to positive transformations of individual or collective behavior. Much the opposite occurs. Retribution causes defensiveness, contempt, anger, and frequently aggression. This is especially true when any one of us or a group of people is in crisis.

Nonetheless the feeling, emotional side of myself finds it easy and necessary to express outrage and disdain for the human forces that I believe support injustice, harm, and in balance, death over life. Nor am I shy when it comes to holding the people and institutions that exert force and power for death responsible for their actions and/or inactions. All the while I am exceedingly aware it is not only "them;" it is also me. I contribute to and am responsible for the conditions I decry. I know in my heart that I'm accountable for finding proactive ways to cope with what, more often than not, overwhelms me; I am accountable for acting in the service of healthy social-political change as best as I'm able; as a person and as a poet.

These are the tensions of social-political reality that I confront... blame and empathy, retribution and responsibility, whining and doing.

If we are to rebirth a future in which our Earth and all that live on it have a genuine opportunity to live a healthy life; a future that serves life, then I believe three actions are essential. First, we must embrace rather than deny the perils we face; second, we must move off the mark of despair, cynicism, and inertia; and third, we must act with courage...with strength, integrity, and forgiveness.

This chapter of Adaptive Tensions *is my humble contribution to support life and foster a positive future; to say, "I have seen the future and it works!"*

What About Our Children?

out they tumble
from Friday afternoon school doors
spilling on to buses and walkways
chattering with friends and holding their parents' hands
the unusually warm fall day
freshens the air with playfulness
out they tumble
nurtured by a carefree moment
smiling with trusting eyes
and an open heart

is there anything we wouldn't do
to protect them from life-threatening illness and harm?
is there anything we wouldn't do
to keep them safe from abuse and hurt?
would we stand by
while they suffocated?
would we watch
while they starved?
would we be at ease
while they died in the streets
no!
certainly not!

out they tumble
nurtured by a carefree moment
unconcerned with our politics and our policies
that support death over life
allowing carbon
to smother our children's breath
allowing millions
to sleep on churning stomachs
allowing just as many
to seek shelter in train tunnels and doorways
and cardboard boxes in rat-ridden alleys

death over life
that allows our children's present and future
to be stolen by greed and war
by inequality
and climate change
stolen, in our full view

out they tumble
is there anything we wouldn't do?

Peace Talks

I bend to meet your downcast eyes
conversations that break down
before they begin
no-win situations
from the very start
when all we want
is a bit of imagination
for the sake of our children
knowing they are secure
where they go to school and pray
protected by the adults who profess their love
the pain-filled screams of rockets raining down
on their helpless heads
leave our hearts in ruin
and despair
drained of a thousand tears
a waterfall over their small graves
all those we cherished
and lost
for what possible reason

I bend to meet your downcast eyes
conversations that break down
before they begin
seeing only the differences
rather than what we share in common
when all we want
is a bit of understanding
for the sake of our children
who die in our arms
without a chance to grow old
the remains of tiny shoes
and shattered dreams
tattered drawings emptied of color
and faces beyond recognition

churning up storms of terror and hate
no light or future in sight
only the past darkness
holding fast to worlds apart
our lives quickly disappearing
with each separate breath

Endless Desire

robots and automatons
feigning empathy and wisdom
artificial intelligence pretending to be human
captured my children
took them to the winter slaughterhouse
where the wolves wear suits and ties
and like to gather at the top of the hill
waiting for their prey
teeth smiling and vicious
dripping saliva mixed with blood
pools of red smoldering in the snow
giving off steam
hot with the fresh
smell of the kill
still hungry for more
the thrill never sated
the wanting to sneer
contempt for the less powerful
the sick and the wounded
feeding the pack's endless desire
for helpless victims

Abandoned

you are abandoned in the denial
of the river dammed at its source
you are abandoned in the vacuum
of the orphan's empty stomach
you are abandoned in the worn-out prayers
of priests and politicians
you are abandoned in the silence
of your blood running cold

Global Warming

saw my children
wandering streets leveled by desolation
searching for a sign of life
clothes tattered and homeless
while I watched from afar

saw my children
bellies bloated with air
picking over garbage dumps
eating termites and tree bark
while I watched from afar

saw my children
covered in dust
mouths bone dry
tongues swollen with thirst
while I watched from afar

saw my children
on fire in the sky
burning up in flames
naked against the sun
while I watched from afar

saw my children
frozen stiff in the ground
fingers and toes blackened by frostbite
hollow screams etched into their faces
while I watched from afar

saw my children
sinking beneath the rising sea
flailing to keep their heads above the waves
gasping for one more breath before going under
while I watched from afar

To Howl With You

I want to howl with you
at the towers collapsing on innocence
on the immigrants from terror and orphaned children
crying for shelter
howl with you at the dust and debris of greed
sealing up firefighters in body-bags
sending them home in pieces
much less than whole
howl with you at happy meals
stuffed down our throats
choking us to death
with super-sized smiles
howl with you at the heartless jackals
sacrificing those we love
on a garbage heap of lies
piled high to the sky
howl with you
at the fear of strange sounding names
spit from our lips
as if they were venom
and might make us ill
howl with you at the master-minds of extraordinary rendition
double-speak alien tongue
for abduction and torture
powerlessness and water boarding
howl with you at the acne-spotted faces
sleeping in tunnels and on benches
covered by yesterday's news
the bold type headlines of their lives growing old
howl with you
at the crippled and shattered
sitting in their own urine, drooling
waiting for the help
that never comes soon enough
or ever at all

howl with you
at the pus-like pity
oozing from every pore of our skin
while dignity lays bound and gagged
face down in the gutter
without a bed to sleep on
howl with you
at the diseased and torn bodies
dangling from flagpoles
uncared for heroes
fighting in a war of survival
howl with you
at the kings and princes of arrogance
gang banging Mother Earth
holding her down against her will
howl with you
at the clowns of consumption
warming the planet beneath a thick blanket of smoke
that keeps out the sun
and makes us shiver in summer
howl with you
at the odds stacked up high
like a pile of writhing worms
feeding on the blood of our children
because there is no tomorrow
they can hold in their eyes

Coincidental Randomness

a ballet slipper in the snow
frozen in a dance of thieves
stealing the future

a cannibal in the 21st century
hungry mad for a morsel of flesh
even his daughter's

a butterfly floating in the sun
her wings on fire
burning up over a sullen earth

a traveler in another time
trapped in the steel-like grasp of hope
wound tight around his chest

a raging bull in the rain
shrinking away from inevitable heartlessness
the deepest distrust

a tree turned upside down in the sky
sap bleeding from her eyes
falling to the ground without a cry

a greedy conference table made of elegant mahogany
clear glasses of water set upon murky agendas
half-empty ideas crowding the air

Naming It

when a country allows its soldiers
to torture and maim
in the name of revenge
and looks the other way
while tens of thousands
are shot through the backs of their heads
when a country ignores the killing of children
and innocence trying to surrender
content to live in denial
in the lies told with the blood
of the vulnerable
all those unable to protect themselves
do we call it war
or murder

when a state permits gold-diggers and profiteers
to pump water without end
keeping secret deals
hidden from its citizens
paying no consideration
to those upon who the state depends
not even a single cent of the taxes paid
yet well aware of the billions earned
at the peoples' expense
white collars taking a pig's share
of the drinkable water on our planet
while children die of thirst
do we call it free enterprise
or murder

when a vigilante
stalks a youth of color
and sends a bullet
through the soft tissue of his chest

the line between reasonable suspicion and paranoia
blurred by seeing only the differences
pushed to the brink by unwarranted fear and hate
both of them standing their ground
trembling in the cold shadows
of a dark rainy night
beyond left and right
and so close to the safety of their homes
do we call it self-defense
or murder

Never Whole Again

another gun
erupting with thunder
spewing flames
an officer's disdain
shining in the daylight
cutting down a boy of color, again
the weight of empty lies
exploding in the street
passionate unrest reaching the boiling point
fists throbbing with revenge and grief
rocks and Molotov cocktails
tear gas and rifle fire
shattered store windows and heads cracked open
sorrow and turmoil
hot tears and cold rage
the mothers and fathers
brothers and sisters
bent in pain
shaking in the night
their lives stolen by hate
and all our hearts broken
never to be whole again

Nooses

to the freeway
where vigilantes ride in the night
crosses burning
nooses trailing behind their pick-ups
wild-eyed, fiery hate fiercely raging
on the lookout for those mongrel dogs
whose bloodline is easily spilled
over years of enslavement
turned artificially sweet by pseudo emancipation
an imagined freedom
from prisons of bigotry and racism
very much alive in the cold hearts
of white minded supremacists
washed clean of guilt
marching to the beat of revelation
and the rapture
of a final solution

Brought to My Knees at Wounded Heart

there is a place of tragedy
where thousands upon thousands of our ancestors
were murdered by other ancestors of ours
this is the place of anger
fear
depression
loneliness
frustration
despair
that finds its way into our homes and relations
killing our better selves
letting out our demons
a place of tragedy
where my heart is cold
and I am brought to my knees

Force Begets Resistance

1.

what courage does it take
for gas moguls and corporateers
to frack deep fissures
poisoning the earth
in the name of green
no courage at all
just vested interest in piracy and profit

what courage does it take
for white collars
to sit safely away
ordering miles and miles of pipeline
in the name of conservation
no courage at all
just singular focus on propaganda and avarice

what courage does it take
for work boots and families of four
to roll up their sleeves and band together
to question and challenge
in the names of their neighbors
more courage than they should bear themselves
to preserve the land that is all of ours

2.

what would occur
if we didn't turn away
surely our jobs
and our livelihood might be at risk
what would occur
if we didn't turn our heads
we would have to choose
fill the streets
or cower in our homes
lock arms in loud resistance
or choose the silence of complicity

what courage does it take
to refuse self-serving authority
what courage does it take
to watch each other's back
what courage does it take
to protect our children
and make them proud

Callous Souls

callous souls
layer upon layer of numbed skin
yellow and bloodless
do not peel away on their own
or feel what is under their step
they march on
deaf to the cries and moans
smothered beneath their boot heels

callous souls
slab upon slab of hardened flesh
crusty and deadened
do not strip away by themselves
or care about who's in their way
they keep rolling on
blind to the fear and terror
crushed under the weight of their wheels

I'm Going Down
(in violence)

I'm going down
to the streets where you hang
drive-by every night
soaking the pavement
with fire and blood
justice fast and right

I'm going down
to the beds where you sleep
shooting up the sky
with rockets and tracers
turning buildings to piles of rubble
and making babies gasp for air

I'm going down
to the alleyways where you hide
raining Sarin over my own
choking off the breath
of the innocent
and the downtrodden

I'm going down
to the hillsides where you farm
machetes slicing off limbs and heads
in the name of rebellion
cleansing the land
with wild-eyed hands of hate

I'm going down
to the village where you pray
set myself ablaze
darkening the day for freedom denied
and for rebirth
with the smell of my burning flesh

I'm going down
to the schools where you feel safe
looking for your children's lives
snuff them out with a smile
stab you in the heart
for no reason at all

I'm going down
to the theaters and malls where you're entertained
lots of guns, ammo, and a bulletproof vest
tickets to heaven's gate
celebrating our belief in violence and terror
so easily in my reach

Assassination
(for Benazir Bhutto)

a little boy
pedals his bicycle furiously across the screen
his right hand wound tightly around the handlebar
his left hand covering his ear
in the background
emergency lights scream and flash
sirens blare distress and fear
rushing to collect the carnage
still laying in the blood-soaked gutter
wailing fist-clenched faces
shocked, sobbing faces
run bewildered down panic filled streets
as if it was their daughter who had been murdered
the breath of chaos
makes the small hairs
on the back of their necks
stand on end

Syria

do you wake up another morning
to his lies
another day listening to the cries
of your children, your loved ones
and those you don't know
beaten and bloodied
wounded and dead in your arms
their future on the run

do you wake up another morning
to the terror he wields
another day discovering
babies buried in mass graves
men bound like pigs
women shot in the head
the stink of death
hovering all around

do you wake up another morning
to the moans and prayers
another day starving
for self-determination
hungry to hear the silence of complicity
broken by the roar of humanity
unwilling to be spectators
any longer

do you wake up another morning
to your sacrifice
another day determined to be alive
no matter what you might have to give
dying on your feet
rather than living on your knees
called to something beyond yourself
freedom, justice, peace

do you wake up another morning
to the helplessness of the world
another day wondering
how we could stand by
witnessing the carnage
bodies strewn like trash on your streets
watching the boot heel of oppression
crushing your breath

do you wake up another morning
ever seeing the end

Unwilling

I was unwilling
to pay the price of lip-service
that jumped around our dinner table
at Thanksgiving

the cost of continuing this war
or bringing our soldiers home
a conversation
which could be heard
around TV's and newspapers and computers
where people were informed of the pros and cons
learned about the sacrifices that would be required
and why they were necessary
a hundred different voices
broadcasting different points of view
too scared to stop the killing
or not scared enough

my uncle Abe knew about war
a medic on Omaha Beach
he had seen it all
he had been it all
all the horror
he didn't talk about it
but you could see it engraved in his face
the crevices and potholes of cynicism and pain
etched in by a white hot blade

and there were my friends, Donny and John
whose bodies and spirits came back from Khe Sanh
numb and lifeless
and soon after, were finally dead
they also hardly talked at all
the misery they saw and participated in
and gave their lives for

kept them quiet
writhing in the privacy of an anguished silence
until they were consumed, overcome
by what they witnessed
and had a hand in

so what do I know about war
how can I talk
about the worthiness of paying the costs
my eyes are not Uncle Abe's
or Donny's or John's
how can I talk about necessity
my knowledge of what we face
is only as good as what I'm fed
the information and the misinformation
the facts and the deceptions
innocently propagandizing a view of truth
that only varies in where it lies
and is impossible for me to assess

I could not pay the cost of lip-service
that jumped around our dinner table
this Thanksgiving
as we sipped hot coffee and tea
and fingered pumpkin pie into our mouths
debate slipped out edge-wise from our tongues
about the necessity of war
about whether or not to pay the costs of war
about which, really
we knew nothing

A Flag in the Window
(Father's Day 2007)

yesterday, while taking a walk on Father's Day
I saw a photograph
covering a neighbor's window
it had been encased in a painful black border
and placed squarely
beneath our flag

I was surprised by how young he looked
a real baby-face
could have been our son's photograph
his flag
that were the only remains
besides the memories of those
who loved him
it could have been our child
who wasn't coming home
who had left for war
like all the others
enlarged in life and death
by their photographs
encased in a painful black border
and placed squarely
beneath our flag

this is what they really mean
when they engage in double-speak debate
about the integrity of the surge
as if it were water or electricity that was flowing
instead of blood

and it isn't only the photographs
of the dead
it's also the ones who come home maimed
and without decent care
strangers to themselves
and so different than those you knew before

perhaps their photographs
should be in the windows
of our homes too
smiling upward upon
the loyalties that betrayed them
in the name of country
the red white and blue
the stars and stripes
that allowed them to be wounded
and hurt
for no reason
and without adequate protection
changing them forever
their photographs
could also line the streets where I walk
on Father's Day
encased in a painful black border
placed squarely
beneath our flag

Have You Come?

have you come to bury me
with bugles in your heart
playing a mournful tune
and your spindly arms
waving frantically goodbye
to places where rotting flesh
rises half mast
embroidered on tear-soaked stars and stripes
to which pledges of allegiance
sound like empty promises
and each coffin stares in vain
at those left behind

have you come to carry me home
with photo albums in your eyes
and your trembling legs
wanting to run far away
to places where your skin smells alive again
like the freshness of truth
for which honor and glory
are worth your sacrifice
and each of the wounded
remembers the dream still to be lived

Saw the News Today

saw the news today
about an American son
held captive for so long
the mission to free him
attempted in vain

saw the news today
about an American son
beheaded by an Englishman
the video sent 'round the world
with a warning of what's to come

saw the news today
about an American son
a family's tears
in all our eyes
falling hard like a bitter rain

saw the news today
about an American son
left in the dust
of a foreign land
never coming home again

All Sides

the beauty in the world
the smile of sunset
the love that fulfills
at a mother's breast
I can imagine
I can savor
but the horrors of my time......
the hate that pollutes
like poisoned run-off
the anger that strikes indiscriminately
like a mad fiend
I find unfathomable
I find impossible
all sides claiming a noble cause
while atrocity flourishes like a weed

Hard Work

1.

keeping the faith
and my door shut tight against cynicism and despair
holding fast to eyes that see opportunity
in every challenge
is hard work
like dealing with the cold of winter
and shoveling snow
like everything in fact,
that becomes harder as I grow older

it's not about being content or satisfied
or filling up the dark vacuum of midnight
with pretty dreams
it's not that simple

to be optimistic, even hopeful
I have to let go of the way in which
what calls itself real
imagines my future
I have to give intense effort
and laser-like focus
opening myself to the possibility of pleasant surprise
belief in joyous unpredictability
and that things can be different
and can be changed for the better
that it's possible
the future can be more than wishful thinking

2.

my wife and children make keeping the faith
being optimistic
my responsibility

without expectation of the effects
simply doing my duty as best I'm able
they don't want me to surrender
or to succumb to feeling it's too late
that I've abandoned the forests, the streams, the rivers,
the oceans, the air
in expressions of helplessness
that I allow my pessimism to accept laying ruin to wild places
until they are beyond repair
that I accept the shearing of mountain tops
for who knows what purpose
besides greed and profit
or that I remain speechless and paralyzed
when our Mother Earth is turned upside down
and inside out

my wife and children look into my eyes
to help them see they're okay
and that our world is sound
they look to me
to fulfill my responsibility
to keep faith in shaping the future
keep the places closest to me
the people closest to me
safe
healthy
protected from harm and damage
and from erosion within

3.

and indeed
I am the steward,
the caretaker of my future
and the future of those I love
so, I am unwilling to sign on the line of least resistance
unwilling to bargain with the power of wealth

the power of oligarchs
the power of the lofty
they are not entitled
to my trust
to ride on the back of my labor
to rape the streams, the rivers, the trees, the mountains
that are my home
my wife's home
my children's home

if the powers that be come to my door
demanding that tomorrow is theirs
I will be quiet in their presence
but not silent
for the beat of my heart
is inseparable from the land
and the quality of my life
inseparable from those I love
this is the courage needed for hope and faith
to lift the weight of despair
and rise-up like the sun

Doing Nothing

I sit in the humid stillness
where nothing moves
not even the air or a cloud
or a bead of sweat
shaded from the hot sun
a poem
like a wave of cool water
washes over me

what might happen
if we had a moment
to listen?
how splendid that might be
freed from the noise
of all the preconceptions and assumptions
the inferences and biases
that separate us
freed from the uneasiness
of all the beliefs and values
that keep us apart
focused on what is different

if we had a moment to listen
only one belief might prevail
belief in one another
only one value might be held close
the valuing of each other

if we had a moment to listen
to the quiet beating of each other's hearts
then surely the homeless would be sheltered
the starving would be fed
the hated would be loved
the wind would give us power
whales and seabirds would be safe
wars would cease
and the world would know peace

when I do nothing
a poem washes over me
everything is possible
we sit together beneath a sturdy tree
arm around one another in a great circle
everything is possible
we stand and walk together
hand in hand with courage and conviction
unanimity without being unanimous
a singular purpose without conformity
life without devastation
everything is possible

when I do nothing
a poem moves inside me
this one
a poem that perhaps
we all might share

Being a Parent

Being the type of parent who builds healthy bonds with my children is my most important and often difficult responsibility to fulfill. I wrote these poems to remind myself of that responsibility and as a source of encouragement as I continue to grapple with the tensions of parenting.

Birth

the boundaries of your legs
widen as far as they can stretch
your muscles push beyond their limits
every sound is a groan

slowly he peaks
making his way into an uncertain world
where mountains and valleys
will soon be his to explore
and the hearts of those he loves
will be elated and broken

born with a silver lining
he smells like morning dew
beckoning to be picked up
and brought back to the sea
from which all of us have come
naked, vulnerable
and without answers

A Child

to see the world
through the laughing yellow light of dandelions
tickling your nose
to see the world
through the rising white mountain snow fort
built with your hands into the wall of a snow bank
to see the world
through the budding silver dance of the full moon
tugging on your heart
to see the world
through the arching scarlet sky of dreams and pure sleep
upon which you rest
to see the world
through the breathing green earth of all things sacred
calling you to stand with them
to see the world
through the decaying grays of broken promises
without feeling cynical or angry
or that right and wrong have been lost
to see the world
through the rust-colored rage of a father's gritted teeth
which you turn into a hug
and hope for a better day
a child

All Our Children

they fall into springtime
with the crocuses
laughing their sides off
the sweet delights of freedom
shining from their sweaty faces
red and salty
on a warm Friday afternoon

they fall into the fragrance
of freshly cut lawns
flying through the air
rolling down the green hills
yearning for unscheduled days to come
and lazy nights
watching the stars and fireflies

they fall into the singing wind
dancing with willows
swaying gently to and fro
keeping the beat
of rhythms that only they can hear
melodies all their own
and theirs to keep

You Are

you are the sun that lights up our eyes
warms our skin
and gives sustenance to our souls

you are the moon that makes us glow
moves us like the ocean tides
and helps us to relax in the flow

you are the Earth through which we become
where we always feel at home
and know we belong

you are the garden from who we grow strong
in whose soil we are born and reborn
and learn to honor Mother Nature

you are the wind chimes that sings us songs
dances in the rain and thunder
and welcomes us into your arms

From You

from you they receive sunshine
when they awake in the morning
your smile to start their day
the taste of dew you kiss onto their lips
and the warmth of your strong arms
that wrap around their small bodies
like the softness of fleece
a sign that they're at home with you
and in the right place

from you they receive
baths filled with bubbles and water toys
that kindles imaginative play
shampoo that turns their hair and bodies
into sweet bouquets
over which you swoon and coo
in grand celebration
as their rollicking giggles
splash over the sides of the tub
and then burst into laughter and joy

from you they receive
shirts, pants, socks and underwear
and other more fanciful gifts
the most precious of which
is the way you make their lives yours
and give your time unselfishly
attending nearly every event
giving witness to their accomplishments
and their hard work
honoring the delicious moments spent snuggling in bed
rubbing their backs
listening to their jokes and stories
their cries for a Band-Aid
and the times when they are angry

from you they receive
your mountain-like presence and spirit
energy to read a book
write a letter to a friend
tackle a puzzle
or work a math problem
energy to ice skate and ski
and to learn how to swim
draw a picture
or sit with you on the floor
playing a game, having fun
from which they gain pleasure
a sense of achievement
and new found power

from you they receive
opportunity to hike steep trails
to smell the trees and the forest floor
to fly on planes to distant places
that perhaps would remain unseen
open to experiences
which might otherwise go unfelt
from where they can see their connection to the earth
and how difference and similarity
make our planet a community

from you they receive nurturance and protection
freedom from hunger
cover from rain and thunder and lightning
comfort from dark cold nights
from which they are nourished
and make friends with their fears
from which they come to understand empathy
their need to share their strengths with others
and muster the courage
to shake hands with change
to embark upon new adventures

moving at their own pace
all important reminders
of the possibilities
that fill their world
encouraging well-calculated risks
and a willingness to try things on their own

from you they receive
the discovery of your own questions
about how the continents of your mind and heart
fit together
your own search for purpose in this life
from which they grow into themselves
learning that it is important
to ask questions about who you are
what you're doing
and what for

from you they receive
a world that makes sense
a nest
from which they can roam
and where they can rest

Thank You

oh mommy
you held us so very close and long
and taught us how to eat and sleep
and walk on our own
all that we needed to learn

oh mommy
you carried us in your womb
and on your breast and back
and kept us safe
always in reach
until we were ready
to be in the world
sometimes very far from home

oh mommy
you wrapped us in your arms
and let us laugh and taste our tears
never rushing in to stop a silly giggle
or treat a scraped knee
so we could discover
what it was like to feel joy and hurt
and soothe ourselves

oh mommy
you picked us up
if ever we took a really hard fall
and cheered us on
through easy days
and those filled with adversity
growing our confidence and self-esteem
like a sturdy maple tree

oh mommy
you helped us find our way
and to keep our balance
when our friends gave little in return
to recognize
lies and truth
weakness and strength
anger and passion
and to know the difference

oh mommy
you showed us how to stand tall
and to tell right from wrong
to keep a keen eye and a strong heart
always alert for injustice
even when it means
needing the courage to be alone

Motherhood

the mischievous rascals of dissolving winter
play tug-of-war with spring
until the game of seasons
leans toward warmth
patient for the sound of wind chimes
gently swinging in the breeze of early May
ringing from the open-sky cathedral
of your motherhood

sacred and overflowing with love
they come to you
giving celebration
to who they are turning to be
on their own now, more and more
revealing only a crescent-moon sliver
of what you are
they remember most
your candle
the soft light of your breast
holding tight with their lips
to the journey they took with you
for months and years
connected at the hip
as some might say, but
all of us in this house know
the attachment is the meshing of souls
and how the world snuggles close at night
so real, so fantastic
from which they receive
their sense of belonging and their freedom
their grounding and their wings
from you
their dear, dear mother
and their best friend

Asleep

I wake up asleep this morning
to give away my son
face strained against the rain
crying in sorrow

my eyes open asleep this morning
to the mayhem of my mind
rivers running in opposite directions
grab for his thin legs
he stares bleakly
already under nourished and numb

my heart is asleep this morning
as I lift him up
I don't care anymore
not enough to save him
seeking relief for my little boy and myself
in the comfort of denial
and the acceptance of irrevocable apocalypse
I wallow in the sludge of cynicism
turning hope into hopelessness

I hold him closely this morning
he smiles, snug and secure
safe and assured
unaware of what is just around the corner
or that I cannot protect him any longer
he looks up at me with complete confidence
cradled in my trembling arms
as I lower him into the abyss
the black hole of missed opportunity
where regret feeds ravenously
on my soul
for all I failed to do

River Talk
(for Jesse)

1.

we talk about parking in the shade
and how hot it's been
we talk about the narrow, overgrown path leading to the river
and the increasing possibility of a tic bite
we talk about where to set down our chairs
and finding a level place shielded from the sun
we talk about the temperature of the water
and if it will feel too cold to swim
we talk about skipping stones
and the kind you need to set a new record
we talk about the music we like
and being excited for our upcoming vacation
we talk about the little things that seem big
an invitation to reach more deeply

2.

we talk about the color of the rocks
and the different tones of sunlight
moving like ghosts through the trees
we talk about your first year at a new school
the highlights and the things that were dreadful
Mrs. Roberts and Miss Allista, Mr. Russell and Ms. Stack
we talk about making friends
who you like and why
and spending time with them this summer
we talk about what you dream for yourself
finding your passion
and learning how to live it
we talk about taking your time
enjoying the trip,
as much as getting where you want to go

and not rushing
we talk about what you're looking forward to
what makes you feel alive
and about going to the edge and staying safe
we talk about today and tomorrow
the need to take well-calculated risks
and putting in the work to do what you love
we talk about family and being best friends
always feeling close to your brother, Micah
and seeing each other through

3.

the water feels like mint on my skin
nearby your smile bobs up and down
swaying happily on the surface
where your feet just touch bottom
a gentle current brushes up against us
taking our conversation downstream
with the wind

Actors' Studio

spurned by the disdain of peers
and the contempt of status-quo mediocrity
bored to death
by vacuous screens
they don masks of foreign characters
occupying a presence
all their own creation
where they are safe behind anonymity
neither understanding nor caring to explain
for fear of abandoning their costume
losing invisibility
the shield protecting their identity
on the sometimes strange stage of middle school

Upon a Rite of Passage
(to Micah on his thirteenth birthday)

1.

Micah, the subjects you study in school, the grades you receive
are rather unimportant
compared to the character of your teachers
the relationships you form
what you choose to master
and the learning you do
that ignites your passions, your dreams
and nourishes you
when there is little else
to hold on to

what you'll do for a living, the amount of money you earn
are small matters
compared to what you call your work
how you make your contribution
and what you see in the mirror
when you have nothing to hide

the way you look, the clothes you wear
hardly count
compared to the promises you keep
to yourself and others
and the empathy you show
confident you'll be okay
and that you'll see others through

the number of rooms in your house, what you have in the bank
are of little consequence
compared to the times that may end empty
and you're alone with yourself
still resilient, hopeful, optimistic
doing what needs to be done
for those you love
including yourself

Micah, measuring yourself next to others
is of little concern
compared to what you ache for in your soul
what you cherish and love
what you're grateful to stand up for
and the risks you're willing to take
opening your arms wide
and sometimes being fooled
yet smiling at the adventure in being alive
daring to imagine
you can fulfill your heart's content

Micah, the way things are, the beliefs you've been given
are pretty meaningless
compared to the way you shape your universe
and if you make a haven
for questioning and curiosity
where you can visit the center of doubt
where you can be deeply wounded by betrayal
yet remain undaunted and unscathed

and whether your friends think you're funny
or quick-witted
isn't much compared to the quiet way you listen
when those you care for feel hurt and sorrow
and need to be heard
in the safety of your strong heart

what you've been told to avoid and fear
isn't important
compared to the courage you muster
to become who you are
to discard all the warnings
about being careful
realistic
mindful of your limitations
and what you can't do
persistent in the pursuit of your dreams

2.

Micah, I believe you'll have good stories to tell me
about the next part of your journey
about the times you defied the disappointment of others
and were true to yourself and your soul
about the times you were able to accept finger pointing
accusations of fault and blame
and what you did to take them in
help them feel at home

I believe you'll have good stories to tell me
about the times you refused to be shackled
by frustration and anger
by failure and defeat
about the times that you held on to your faith in yourself
and met people you could trust
who stood in the center of fire with you
back to back

Micah, I believe you'll have good stories to tell me
about the times you danced with things wild
inside and out
and played and sang in joyful celebration
happy that you were alive
about the times you experienced beauty
were present in beauty
knew the peacefulness of beauty
were nurtured by the sacred
and the transcendent
and felt its source in yourself
shouting "Yes!!!"

Loving

I'm convinced that all kinds of "being in love", experiencing oneness and fulfillment with another person, is periodic and oscillates at varying frequencies. Loving and being loved often feels ecstatic, quiet…blissful. But there are also periods when our love relationships feel splintered and ugly. Being in love is a balancing act of taking and giving, selfishness and sacrifice, holding fast to our expectations and loving unconditionally. Keeping these opposites in balance so that our love relationships are renewing and support personal and mutual growth is adaptive tension.

Ponderings on Duality
(an anniversary poem concerning oneness)

to let go and to have
to hold and to be free
to live and to die in the same breath.........

to be the moment before thunder
when you enter any room
rolling through the sky
where twelve mourning doves talk
and sit in quiet contemplation of their song

to be the rustling of the wind
when you enter any place
resting on the sound of the water
where twelve rivers run with laughter
and with loads that are sometimes too heavy to carry

to be the mist at dawn
when you enter any heart
awakening tired flowers and hummingbirds
where twelve trees grow their roots deeply
and there's more they need to take from the earth

to be an artisan's steady hand
when you enter my soul
stirring the child in me, fast asleep
where twelve monks sculpt who we are always becoming
and the selves from which we hide.........

to let go and to have
to hold and to be free
to live and to die in the same breath

On the Day You Were Born

on the day you were born
no one knew the wisdom you would bring
and not a flower could be grown
as fragrant as yours

on the day you were born
no one knew the compassion you would show
and not a mountain could rise
as tall as yours

on the day you were born
no one knew the challenges you would own
and not a story could be told
as bravely as yours

on the day you were born
no one knew the secrets you would reveal
and not a truth could be held
as honestly as yours

on the day you were born
no one knew the prayer you would share
and not a river could run
as deeply as yours

on the day you were born
no one knew the choices you would make
and not a voice could be heard
as strong as yours

on the day you were born
no one knew how you would make the Earth move
and not a revolution could turn
as passionately as yours

on the day you were born
no one knew the music you would become
and not a song could be sung
as sweetly as yours

A Valentine's Gift

you tell me
it's an early Valentine's gift
a surprise
a new quilt cover
to replace our tired and worn one
"your favorite colors," you say
but to me,
the motley colored greens
feel pale and out-of-place

I detest green

"it feels scratchy, I say,
not soft, like our old one
it feels like the wool pants I had to wear
when I was twelve"
"it will get soft," you say
but I've already waited long enough

"it's a metaphor, you say,
for what we might restore
kinder words
protecting what's important"

but all I feel
is a metaphor
for one more decision
made without me
one more expression of your power and presence
one more time for you to exercise control
pushing your weight around

I detest green

Your Eyes

crystals of rain-frozen ice
glisten in the thin smile of moonlight
the path leading from the mudroom
lights up with hope
reminding me of your dazzling eyes
burning
deep and red-hot
against the dark background of night
showing us our way
through perilous terrain

Join Me in March

join me in March
take your angry weather
out on me
the drab grays and browns
waiting for the hope of spring
grown impatient and powerless
on its long way to our door

join me in March
take your cold chill
out on me
the piercing damp grimaces
knowing the first signs of growth
are far away
holding their breath

join me in March
take your weary heart
out on me
the rusted hinges breaking apart
from the slurs and shouting
glad we can slam doors
in each other's faces

A Simple Heart

this evening
a simple heart comes to you
to find and give shelter
from the loneliness we sometimes feel
a simple heart
rising over our barbed-wire thoughts
and the vengeance we sometimes imagine
a simple heart
open and faithful, beating strong

this evening
a simple heart comes to you
singing softly in your ear
listening carefully to our voices
a simple heart
keeping his words plain and easy
like the kiss of a snowflake
a simple heart
on fire in the frozen sky

this evening
a simple heart comes to you
laughing at the secrets we hide
only for our lips to shape
a simple heart
gathering us close to the edge
fear and anticipation burning us up
a simple heart
passions still smoldering in the night

Passive Aggression
(1993)

when do we learn to turn the screw?
wearing an artificial smile
beyond being questioned
claiming nothing is wrong
how do we learn to ask rhetorical questions?
pretending there is more than one answer
such insincerity
knowing there's only a single response
where do we learn to control our rage?
beneath the love we profess
conducting a cold war
as if everything was fine

I wonder, do we realize
how we fool ourselves
how fearful we are
of uncovering our untruths
and self-deceptions
thinking and acting as if we're satisfied
when we're not
searching for a river that has mostly run dry
little joys and pleasant reminders
of what once was
hardly any faith in restoration
so we express our entrapment
passive aggression
blaming and finding fault
with our hands behind our backs
scapegoating each other
without recognizing the harm

I wonder
when do we learn to live
crawling on our hands and knees

But Me

honey,
the rain swallows up the sky
but me
I'm dry beneath the canopy
we've built
branch by branch
strong hand by strong hand
trusting hearts
loving souls

sweetheart,
the lightning tears up the sky
but me
I'm safe on the mountain
we've climbed
rock by rock
strong hand by strong hand
trusting hearts
loving souls

darling,
the thunder explodes in the sky
but me
I'm quiet in the calm
we've created
soft step by soft step
strong hand by strong hand
trusting hearts
loving souls

angel,
the wind blows cold in the sky
but me
I'm wrapped snug in the warmth
we radiate
fiery embrace by fiery embrace
strong hand by strong hand
trusting hearts
loving souls

Forced to Lie

it would be easier to put my lies on you
to dress you in them
make you wear them
like a disguise
when really they are mine
that clothe me
and I am the fugitive
from truth
denying responsibility
for the fictions I create
blaming you for my fantasies
the myths my ego conjures and concocts
when I am the escapee
the refugee fleeing reality
bound tightly in self-fulfilling prophecy
and the dismal gray sadness
knowing I am fooling myself

In Tandem

1.

If I Didn't Know Better

if I didn't know better
I might think you came to me
from another planet
the distance you traveled
so far and in between
such great courage and endurance
to traverse the distant boundaries
of past lives
satisfying a hunger to be free

if I didn't know better
I might think you came to me
from another universe
the time I waited
so long wrestling with sorrow
the emptiness and loneliness I kept
raging, aching hours
crying for you to arrive
begging for a miracle

if I didn't know better
I might think you came to me
from another world
the wisdom you give away
so rich and filling
the light and warmth in which I wake
laying naked in the softness
of a fairy tale
listening to you sleep

2.

Fairy Tale

fairy tale
where do you take me
across the ocean in your smile
and the moonlight pouring through your hair
where I live among your Tulips
that bloom outside our door
protecting my heart
from wind and whim
where I live
among your gardens
and the trees you've planted
basking in the rain and sunlight
of your earthy brown eyes
where I live in the sanctuaries you've built
giving your soul to peace
and growth
and to me
in a fairy tale

Leaving

you can go where you want to
land with thunder on my chest
grit your teeth and clench your fists
but you can't pound the light anymore

you can do what you want to
crash into brick walls
flail like a windmill in the driving wind
but you can't pretend you care anymore

you can say what you want to
fake your love and talk up the lies
cower and tell me you'll change
but I can't risk staying anymore

you can cry and shriek if you want to
call it your last breath
name it mercy for what it's worth
but you can't keep what you haven't got

In the Time that Remains

in the time that remains
I need your smile
to shine a light
and welcome the sky
I need your eyes
to see today and tomorrow
and show me my way
I need your kiss
to wake the morning
and wish me goodnight
I need your strength
to lift me up
and carry me through
I need your embrace
to send my fears away
and tell me everything's all right

in the time that remains
I need your love
to hold on to
and to keep out the cold
I need your love
to wrap around my heart
and make me snug and warm
I need your love
to find peace
and fill the missing part of my soul

Reminders at Night

the times you snore
with loud gusts of wind
or moan in the nightmare
you're running from

the times you lay diagonally
heating up my side of the bed
or when you toss and turn
shaking the creaks from the mattress frame

the times you walk to the bathroom
feet pounding hard against the floor
or roll out the toilet paper
rumbling like thunder from our grumbling dispenser
always wake me up
reminding me you're alive
and in my life
like the reassuring smile of sunrise
sweeping away the uncertainty
of this anything-can-happen life

August

in the languishing heat of August
we find shelter in the cool of night
and the promises made beneath our huppa
sacred vows given and received
our road to the future
and each other
renewed on this summer day
every year
never forgotten or forsaken
or taken for granted

in the languishing heat of August
we find shelter in the cool of night
and the celebration held in our hearts
precious gem-like moments given and received
our light through hard times
reclaimed on this magical day
every change of August to September
always held close and revered
reminder that life transforms

in the languishing heat of August
we find shelter in the cool of night
and the oneness in which we rejoice
another tomorrow given and received
our story still to unfold
and to record on our own
the start of a new chapter
with every passing day
always being written and read
and turning another page

September Surrounds You

September surrounds you
balancing you in the embrace
of your garden's last birth
and the trees first to turn

September bounces you on her knee
singing to you in kind reflection
of the places that mark your face
and the new paths you'll carve
to planned and unknown destinations
sharing in their anticipation
of rediscovery and strengthened understanding

September explores with you
setting foot upon past landmarks
and venturing into the next season
searching for just the right questions

September catches her breath with you
letting you rest on her pillow of clouds
soft, like the memories of good times
hard, like the setbacks you recall
holding in common
the trust
that sun and moon will always rise
one self
shining and reflecting
one revolution
dancing arm in arm
one turn more
in harmony with the beginning of another year

Attention

in my dream
a midnight moon
rang from a distant clock tower
circling below
you danced among a gathering of candles
your arms raised in welcome
to thoughtful owls
and wolves wishful for the hunt
a gust of wind swirled and twisted
sending the first leaves of September into the air
wood nymphs and elves joined in celebration
traditional gifts were transcended
and the boundaries of time abandoned
something far beyond the ordinary
beckoned
something deeper, more intense, more meaningful
something infinite
called to me
focusing my attention
on the orange light of autumn
glimmering in your tender eyes

Your Virgo Moon

your Virgo moon ignites the midnight sky
fire-starter of yet another year
a time to rekindle your curious nature
and taste raindrops on your tongue
a time to renew your attraction to daybreak
and be thrilled by the sound of rolling thunder
a time to seek new adventures
and make use of stories you've been told
a time to keep your door wide open
and welcome in miracles to uplift your heart
a time to follow your own compass
and to remember to trust yourself on the way

your Virgo moon ignites the midnight sky
fire-starter of yet another year
a time to stretch the boundaries of convention
and nourish your imagination
a time to rebirth the mission of your soul
and to grow young rather than old
a time to listen to the harmony of your inner voices
and to work at keeping them in balance
a time to feel that everything is possible
and better understand the purpose you hope to fulfill
a time to hear the cries of life and death
and sing songs of transcendence

your Virgo moon ignites the midnight sky
fire-starter of yet another year
a time for celebrating where you've been
and the places visited
a time for gazing at the horizon
and charting your course ahead

To Free Her Soul

down to the river
storm clouds disappearing in her eyes
the only one left to hold onto
she steps easily through mud-soaked earth
stripped of vulnerability
she comes
naked and open
unclothed and inviting
down to the river
to swim in the moonlight
rushing through her hair
the only one left to hold onto
riding bareback upon unicorns and rainbows
exploding with the fragrance of fresh fruit
she comes
transparent and cloaked
visible and hidden
down to the river
to free her soul
from the sweaty heat of summer

Ours to Keep

your laughing Buddhas
warm the spirit of every season
your angels and the shining sun
rise up high in the sky
your egret and rabbit
stand patiently still
your stars circling the moon
and your graceful swan
smile upon us
protect us
always

your belief in yourself
held close against your breast
your belief in fantasy
in magic and make believe
in the power of prayer
and faith
brings us safely home
opening doors
welcoming the future
with a lingering kiss

your unwavering love
and devotion
like the strongest metal
your hard work
and the empathy in your heart
like the softness of a rose petal
your hope and strength
and your tender caress
filling up the days
passing so quickly by
but forever ours to keep

Upward

I hear your voice
calling me to a place I've never been
where purple and orange ribbons
swing me in the air
while lifting slowly upward
my head tumbles backward
in the fresh smell of rain
in the peace of your smile
that fills the sky above

Home

I lay on the sofa we purchased
looking into the family room we made
and then all the way through the entry
to the large double windows
on the other side of our house
the once empty spaces
filled now
with the laughing dance of children
with photographs of our lives together
with little, story-teller knick-knacks
and the warmth of a piano
filled now
with the plants you grow
with the flowers you arrange
with the colors you love
with the aroma of your sweat
and tears
with the starlight of your strong eyes
and playful heart
home

If I Could

if I could
I would take your lead wherever it might go
hold your hand every step of the way
through shadow and light
just to be with you

if I could
I would climb the tallest mountains with you
swim with you across raging rivers
listen to the things most difficult to hear
just to be with you

if I could
I would keep to the path you've made
always by your side
with my arm around your waist
just to be with you

and if I could
I would dream the dream in your eyes
rest my head against your breast
feel each beat of your heart
just to be with you

Come Knock On My Door

when your heart is drowning in sadness
and weariness
and your body aches
come knock on my door
I'll be holding a candle for you
reaching out my hand
to help you find your way
from bitter cold and winter gray
a better, easier place to be

when your heart crawls inside itself
and you wish you could hide
on the dark side of the moon
come knock on my door
I'll be holding the sun for you
opening my arms wide
to offer refuge
sanctuary from the numb and uncaring
a warmer, safer place to be

when your heart swims across the sky
and every bit of you is alive
with exhilaration
come knock on my door
I'll be holding a celebration for you
the music you like best
and all those you love
dancing on a mountaintop
a fresh and inspiring place to be

when your heart lifts up the stars
and spreads their light
way across the heavens
come knock on my door
I'll be holding a mirror
and the reflection of your smile
to help you see yourself
as all you are
a powerful, enchanted place never very far

Will You?

will you let me woo you one more time?
being the person who you love the best
will you let me sweep you off your feet again?
being the person who excites you the most
will you let me make you shudder with delight as I used to?
being the person who touches the deepest joys of your heart
will you?

A Lover's Note

mountain skies in your dreams tonight
the heartbeats of a racing pulse
rich dessert tingling on your tongue
waking morning's light

liquid shadows in your dreams tonight
steaming moon before you sleep
rising dawn of delight
slow dancing with a velvet tide

a torrid breath in your dreams tonight
sighing on your skin
simple pleasures to enjoy
casting a lover's charm

baby steps in your dreams tonight
rushing to an open door
no time to hesitate
or resist anymore
or resist anymore

Yearning

will I be ready some day
to be swept off my feet
cradled in your arms of surprise
and sweet surrender

will I be ready some day
to be taken far out to sea
ride a rip-tide with you
to an island in the sky

will I be ready some day
to find my way
to your enchanted place
where every fruit tastes like a first kiss

will I be ready some day
to drink the nectar I once knew
let my lips rest upon yours
and tingle with bliss

will I be ready some day
to be brought to my knees
poised at the edge of your delight
an oasis where I can satisfy my heart's content

will I be ready some day
to hold the moment of risk and fantasy
when you took my breath away
and life was full and so very easy

The Seasons
(an anniversary poem)

the seasons of our love
have no names
nothing to separate them
or box them in
they are joined together seamlessly
across the imperceptible motion of a rainbow
shimmering with only the slightest undulations
like a child deeply asleep
dreaming intimate encounters
where we are safe in our hearts
free from the bondage of insecurity

the seasons of our love
have no time
nothing to make them hurry
or lose their breath
they are embraced in each other's arms
beyond measurement and divided space
moving steadily through the universe
where we learn to read our changing rhythms
like an ever-evolving species
living our lives in the balance
adapting our steps forward
as we pass places we've been before
and move on
free of pretension
about the future we are shaping as ours

Loving You

1.

the fragrance of fresh tomatoes
drenched in the sweat of your garden
drifts upward from your smooth skin
opening the night to my senses

2.

loving you is endless
like the sky and stars
and the storms that arise from nowhere
loving you is without any regrets
like the forgiveness of a child
after battles raged with thunder and lightning
loving you is infinite
like life and death
without borders to hold me back or in
where rivers are crossed beneath moonlight
showing me the path
that leads to your door

3.

I do not love you as a moth loves a flame
or fire loves the wind
I do not love you without resistance to your charms
or deflecting the arrows you send from Cupid's bow

I love you in the secrets
I dare tell only to you
I love you in the filtered light of late afternoon
when the sun interrupts rain clouds
I love you in the places flowers find shade
and hide from view
I love you in the unspoken words
forgotten by silence

I love you easily
without needing to know from where it comes
or why
I love you humbly
knowing how lucky I am
to be loved in return
I love you not caring
where I end and you begin
I love you feeling your breath as mine
I love you so closely
that when you cry
my eyes fill up with tears

I love you

Forever Totem

on winter nights
we fall into the phases of the moon
they shine through our window
peeking playfully from behind the blinds
and rise into daylight like a flame
quietly marking the infinite passage of time
gently tugging on our fingertips
to join them
past, present, and future lives
seamlessly entwined
made of the strongest, softest cloth
that ever touched our skin
or comforted our hearts
which for me
stands as a totem
giving meaning to forever

I'm Waiting for You

you will probably think
I'm gone
that I left forever
but I'm waiting for you
waiting to move on to our next life
to take another turn in your arms
waiting to fulfill the needs
for which I didn't have time
waiting to hold your hand
to dance another round
waiting to complete what I didn't become
waiting for the moment in our next life
when the present is a foggy past-life memory
which at times feels so clear
I'm waiting for you

A Miscellaneous Life

To Tell the Truth

in the telling of the truth
that traces its way upon paths taken
my story is written
as it really was...........
I recall times when I was overwhelmed
sinking beneath waves ridden with fury
I recall times when I was changed
soaring high in a cloudless sky
and by the telling, by the writing
I am changed again

The Fullness of Emptiness

emptiness abounds with the flickering of fireflies
and the sounds of tree frogs serenading their mates
memories of my childhood fill the night
with the taste of ocean salt
and the crashing of waves upon the shore
emptiness quivers and shakes from the pull of the moon
a silent chorus sings lyrical delight
asking intangible questions
about the essence of life
and the secrets I keep from myself

Evolution

1. Overture

like all my poetry
and my life,
perhaps all of our lives,
darkness mixes with light
thorns with rose petals...
the celebration prevails!

2. Growing Up Inane and Senseless

blue eyes
looking back
on heroes riding into the sunset
imagining what I might become
childhood ideals and dreams
vibrant and alive
slowly crushed beneath the boot heels of hypocrisy
smothered by my two-faced parents and teachers
who preached about another world
and transcendence
but lived only for the lies of the flesh
who pumped ice-water into my veins
tried so hard to make me numb
like them
whipped up blame and anger
that spread like wildfire
in my lost, wandering soul

sunday school nightmares
seep into my sleep
public school drill sergeants scream for obedience
while I worry about grades
how I compare
and coming of age

held prisoner by god and fear
and everything chocolate
carefully measured and doled out
to make me forget the daily news
the pockmarked plains and mountaintops
harboring silos of nuclear destruction
the poor and downtrodden, only a few blocks away
who once were filled with promise and surprise
but now, hardened by futility
into clumps of lifeless clay
barren and desolate

I am held prisoner
by temptation
and every fifteen year-old impulse
held prisoner by the tabloid guardians of the truth
and self-absorption
to make me forget the daily news
the cities left unattended and in decay
the stench of sewers overflowing
and garbage left to rot
make me forget the desperateness and disillusionment
brandished on billboards predicting the future
but I choose my future
I am the future

3. Introspection

I cross the barbed wire into spring
into the freshness of morning dew and newly cut grass
I cross the border into spring
where the animals are still untamed
and those who live there
play and read and sing
and eat ceremonial mushrooms
opening doors of perception
to a hidden, sacred paradise

the music and colors
of oneness-with everything humility
harmony and timelessness
a thousand questions
driving a steady, pounding, exhilarating beat
calling up joy and bliss
......and contempt and despair
my dissatisfaction with self
clawing at the walls
of a wavering, brittle conscience
that finally collapsed and shattered
bent-down too far trying to fit-in
gave too much trying to be liked, accepted
too much to belong to the club
sold out to the material world
got busy gathering up attachments
in return for artificial security
glittering insincerity and dishonesty
meager substitutes for genuine caring and love
I was seduced nonetheless
wore my ego like a crown
that became a heavy burden
wearying and painful to carry

sold out to pain relief
swallowed one kind after another
to get me through
to make me disappear
like a ghost, a phantom
escape from my need to point my finger
to accuse and blame
escape from the hopelessness of love and rejection
of having to cope with loss, guilt, devaluing
abandonment and rage
all the while, surrounded
by a planet crying in grief
forgotten, alone

caught in the jaws of denial
affirming guns and despots
executions and self-righteousness
the distance separating the ragged and the well-dressed
affirming the deep scars
carved into the beautiful face of our mother Earth
and the poisons shoved down her lovely throat
her cries reminding me
there is nowhere to run

4. Redemption

there's nothing that's impossible
nothing that can't be overcome
when you join hands
and step into the light
of another world
committed to making a difference
certain the outcome doesn't matter
only doing what you hope is just and right
for living and let live
the small things and the bigger ones
conserving what we can and occupying the streets
regardless of the odds
or the costs to be paid
open-armed to the sacrifices to be made
giving up what we want
for what we need
no other way
for our children to have a chance of being free
to be safe to sit under the sky
and drink the water
eat the food and swim in the river
break the chain of what someone else thinks they should be
freed from the untruths
blaring into their brains
told a thousand different ways

over and over again
the static and noise holding on tight
gripping their hearts
only to be shaken loose by grit and
mountain-like determination
shaken loose by courage
shaken loose by letting go
shaken loose by the graciousness of love

5. Saved By Love

saved by your crazy love
saved by your crazy, hopeful, love
saved by your eyes and poetry
saved from going home alone
worrying I wasn't good
or enough
saved to lay with you
to share our lives
the struggles and the triumphs
the times we held our heads in shame
and the times we forgave
keeping our promise to see each other through
life after life
and even in death
even in heartache
the emptiness of clothes hanging in the closet
and the pictures on the walls
the cold sleeves of a jacket gone limp
and the laughter overcome by tears
the silence of unanswered questions and faith
swirling in the mystery of the unknown
sharing the air we breathe
impossible to be away from you now
impossible to be close by
unsoothed, even in the light
except by time

6. Finale

my hometown was built inside a poem
the place I was really born
down and out with the rest
pretending to be someone else
until I found myself
understood the myth
and knew what I'd need in my next life...
to hear, feel the strength
of all our voices
rising together so kind and sweet
with no regrets
for heroes buried in the earth
for what we lost
for what we missed
or left undone
because we did our best
to carry on
to see the world in each other
what we could become within ourselves
and together
reaching for the crescendo
heard in the deepest quiet
of a last breath
rippling across the sea
sure to return
again and again

Holding My Stomach In

I've been holding my stomach in
since I was in sixth grade
looking overweight, looking fat
was like facing death
so I wore my ducktail shirts over my pants
and held my stomach in to hide my waist
held it tight
in an anal-retentive vise
that has girdled me ever since
holding in for dear life
holding in for a mirror image that is lean, acceptable, safe
at the expense of self,
which in time
transformed into saving,
conserving, delaying gratification
for some future moment
a moment that can't be realized
indeed, eludes me, precisely because
I hold my stomach in
and time
a future moment that is always too late

Keeping Lists

1. Benefits and Costs

I love lists
I love checking-off the things I've done
crossing them out one by one
done, gone
so gratifying
delicious

I love my lists
I love not having to think;
about what I need to do
I just look at my lists
all the while the future repeats the past
stares back at me
sadly predictable

2. Who Does the Keeping?

I keep records
indexes
inventories
eight or nine different kinds
everything I deem important
the contents of all my professional and personal files
the items and books stored on my office shelves
so I can easily find things I rarely use or even think about
safe from the worry they might get lost
and part of my life with them

I keep lots of lists
what to do when
what to buy at the market
what to remember
where I need to go
who to call a friend
I wonder, who is doing the keeping
me or my lists
I wonder
what is being kept

3. How I Weed

I place a check-mark
in the corner of the things I use
and next to the things I do
I add items that are new
and put a line through those that are dead
everything without a check-mark goes
the multitude of papers I can abandon
the book I intended to read for years
the trip I promised myself I'd take
the names of people I never see or talk with
so many lives that have passed

4. The Challenge of a Foolish Notion

it's quite a challenge
to let go
of the need to hold on
the need to keep things
I'll never need, use, or do
just in case
just in case

it's quite a challenge
to forsake the artificial security
that soothes me into thinking
life is in order
moves in sequence
possesses logic
can be organized
rather than being random, irrational, absurd
that it won't slip away
that it can be saved
and embraced at a later time
quite a foolish notion

Redemption

I wrote this poem
and hope you won't find it strange
it's about another life so far away
it's about the love
I once had
and the memories hanging around
even after all this time

I wrote this poem
and hope you won't find it strange
it's about what we dared to live
it's about the tears
I sometimes shed
and the keepsakes I saved
even after all these years

I wrote this poem
and hope you won't find it strange
it's about a future that was ours
it's about the dreams
I let go of
the ones you wouldn't want me to hold onto
the ones you wouldn't want me to grieve

I wrote this poem
and hope you won't mind
it's about the sadness I left behind
it's about the things I can't change
not being with you
when perhaps I should have
not seeing my reflection in your eyes
or kissing you gently goodbye
forgiving myself and accepting yours
redemption after all this time

We Are Growing Older
(to Linda and Amy)

we are growing older
you, me, and all our friends
our tear-filled memories hidden
beneath desperateness and pain
our stories untold
shut tight behind closed doors
that perhaps could be opened
to help us better understand
the moment in our youth
when life became so very strange

we are growing older
you, me, and all our friends
keeping secrets we dare not tell
even to ourselves
our lips sealed in silence
our ears unable to hear
the unspoken conversations
that perhaps could explain
the moment in our youth
when life became so very strained

we are growing older
you, me, and all our friends
still on guard for the times long ago
the sorry moment in our youth
we prefer not to recall
when we were panic-stricken and abandoned
found it easier
to live in denial
that perhaps now
we might let go of

we are growing older
you, me, and all our friends
the years turned gray and hazy
the days when we couldn't carry on
holding fast to anything we could find
to keep us sane
make sense of the absurd
a mountain of grief standing between us
that perhaps we hoped
would someday be overcome

Driven to the Ground

the rain drives to the ground
in stinging cold torrents
November is coming
dressed in the barren pain
of browns and grays
as the days grow darker
and daylight savings is still far,
far away

Saved for Spring

the leak from the bathroom faucet
drips into my brain
disturbing my sleep at 3:00 a.m.
clamoring for my attention
along with the toilet that won't stop running

the mailbox swings and clangs in the wind
smashing mercilessly against the fencepost
that stands rotted and decrepit in March mud
they whine impatiently to be repaired
to be shown a bit of care

winter bears down, holding on
refusing to leave
frost gathers on the window pane
shutting out the meager light
of a day dressed in gray

I wonder how much longer the air will be cold
and raw
when I'll see a robin, a crocus
or just a patch of blue in the sky
and if I'll be saved for spring

A Long Winter

the unrelenting wind blows hard
bristling
across the scraggly bearded field
crisp, fresh air crackles on the limbs of spruce
bowing humbly
beneath the weight of new snow
sunlight streams between tufts of grey clouds
like the fingers of a hand
spread wide and welcoming
shadows and light dancing
swinging round 'n' round
it's all marvelous, exquisite, splendid...
...but it's also cold
a shivering nineteen degrees
and four inches covering the frozen ground
on this mid-April morning
I know not to be surprised
I live in Vermont
even so,
winter has been here long enough
it's time for spring
time for the hills and fields
to turn green and bright yellow
time to sweat replacing fencepost
splintered and uprooted by ice heaves
time to edge along the flower garden
get my hands dirty in the dark-brown soil
waiting in anticipation
as are we
for signs of new life

Without Lilacs

a spring without lilacs
without the fragrance of lavender
and the rich aromas of purple and pink
winter and summer take turns
visiting during the night
a confused look on their faces
not knowing whether to come or go
winter decides to stay awhile
surprising unsuspecting buds with penetrating frost
dormant jewels
suspended in the uncertainty of a schizophrenic season
torn down by soaking rains
they lay across the cold ground
lifeless and unborn
but promising to return

If Not for the Warmth of Friends and Those I Love
(to Kevin and Michelle)

if not for the warmth of friends
and those I love
for the graciousness of your kitchen
the smell of good food
and the nurturance you bring to the table
from which to sustain the long haul,
the winter would otherwise be too cold
impossible to endure

if not for the warmth of friends
and those I love
for our family room overflowing with conversation
our glasses sweetened with empathy and passion
and the hope made real by action
from which dreams are realized,
the winter would otherwise be too cold
impossible to endure

if not for the warmth of friends
and those I love
for the music in your hearts
the sunlight in your souls
and the quiet of silent contemplation
from which imagination grows,
the winter would otherwise be too cold
impossible to endure

if not for the warmth of friends
and those I love
for the courage you wear
your understanding of strength and integrity
and the work ahead
from which our children shape the future,
the winter would otherwise be too cold
impossible to endure

if not for the warmth of friends
and those I love
for the freedom to be myself
held gently in your smile
and the embrace that reassures
from which family derives meaning,
the winter would otherwise be too cold
impossible to endure

Falling Rainbow

early this evening
a late summer rain
pouted and cried
and when she was done
left us a bouquet of flowers
a crisp double rainbow
hanging on a steel blue sky
suspending our imagination
as we always do
when we see a rainbow

early this evening
a late summer rain
complained and whined
it was too hot
and when she was done
poured us a pitcher-full
of sweet tasting colors
to quench our thirst
as we always do
when our vision is parched

September Window

I see you
looking out your September window
at the gardens
to which you've given your soul
the wheelbarrow filled with tired flowers and vegetables
that won't be invited to our table
bound for the compost instead

I see you
looking out your September window
at the gardens
to which you've given your soul
the orange ribbons still blowing in the wind
the aluminum pans to frighten deer
fast asleep on the ground

I see you
looking out your September window
at the gardens
to which you've given your soul
the last of sunflowers bowing their heads
cloves of garlic and baskets of potatoes
napping in the shed

your September window
beckoning the fall
you so adore
cooler nights and geese in flight
a hot cup of tea and carrot soup
simmering on the stove
warming your hands and heart

your September window
looking out upon hills of fire
and the lawn bearded in frost
notice to roll-up the hose
and shut-off the water
while darkness patiently waits for daylight saving
and the caress of your winter quilt

At This Time of Year

at this time of year
your garden
looks back at me
like the full moon
emptied of any discernible life
hiding the secret
of power and growth
illuminating a brisk November evening

Passages

1.

I remember your voice on my answering machine
the dread lurking behind your calm
something bad seeping from your throat
unusual for you to call me
I picked up the phone immediately
and pressed your number
only to get your machine

I left my own message
"if she is out, perhaps nothing's wrong," I thought
I hoped
wanting my premonition to be mistaken
moments later the shrill ring of the phone
shattered the quiet
and the agonizing news squeezed out from your chest

2.

I wonder where you find the strength
to tell Roy
to make the calls
to take care of the details
to maintain your composure

I wonder where you find the strength
I know what it's like to feel as if your body
was turned inside out
my heart remembers well
waiting for Ellen to come home
to be safe and sound in my arms
waiting to wake from what could only have been a horrible dream

I wonder where you find the strength
to bear the crippling thought of him laying on the floor
alone in his office
what was his last glimpse before his eyes closed shut
his last thought
his last fear

I wonder where you find the strength
to sit in the empty echoes of his voice
and overcome the shadows left behind
to miss his feet crossing the floor
and feel the rustling of the covers
to hear the silence of morning sounds from the bathroom
and see the clothes waiting to be worn
to take his laundry from the dryer
along with the plans forever undone

3.

it is many weeks now
I could count them
but for what purpose

I'm sitting at my computer
where your hands touched the keys
as much your computer as mine
your touch everywhere
the keyboard, the mouse, the monitor, the router
your soft, sock covered steps
leading up the stairs to my office
imprinted in my sight
and downstairs in the den
your face reflects from the screen of my new plasma TV
that you researched
and connected to its stand only a couple of weeks ago
while the Blu-Ray waits for you
remember
we had rescheduled breakfast for that Sunday
just two days away
we were going to install the player and fine tune the TV
remember

only plastic and metal and wires and chips
the Blu-Ray does not understand that you are not coming
but nor do I
my heart curdles in disbelief
in denial
trembling with shock and fear

March 28th
(for Ron McKinnon)

on the birth day soon to arrive
drawing near
with every breath
we are reminded of another birth
and of a life
so very full
yet incomplete
in the hearts of those he loved

The Violence of Butterflies

the violence of butterflies
assaults the lining of my stomach
fluttering with unfathomable sadness
another anniversary of death
at precisely the same time of year

Too Many People

I have known too many people
with whom I shared life
gone, like a shooting star
long before their time
for reasons impossible to understand
beyond the mind
senseless and absurd
killed by a driver asleep at the wheel
heart failure on a honeymoon run
suicide having been lost in war
dead while mowing the lawn
sprawled cold behind an office door
broken in pieces
while bicycling on a country road

too many people
life taken-for-granted
for whom I lit a candle
in homage to the young smile
that I thought would always be
for whom I held the hands
of sisters and brothers
mothers and fathers
sons and daughters
giving tribute to what had been given
and taken too soon
too many people
for whom death came seeking
much too early
too many people
for whom my whole world
cried

After Shock

the eye of your soul goes blind
shattered by the too-soon-to-be-true
the random, absurd waste
of life not lived
a partner and best friend forever
gone so very young
I do not have to imagine
the senseless death of a loved one

it is not the first night in bed alone
or the first walk you take by yourself
that makes you quiver
but soon thereafter
the waves of aftershock make you writhe
your body turns into a knuckle-white fist
gripped by cold and darkness
struggling to hold on, to be composed
in the face of your greatest fear

but the tremors are like an earthquake
the first aromas of fresh-cut grass
only you can smell
the first reds and yellows of fall
only you can see
the first taste of cold air
on your lips alone
the first holiday
spent on your own
the first birthday
absent of gifts to give
the first anniversary
with only yourself to hug
the clothes still folded
looking out from the dresser draw
the first step into the future

the tremors are like an earthquake
they wail deeply inside
shock wave after shock wave
breaking your heart into pieces
like ice snapping frozen tree branches
until in time
long as it may be
the tremors subside
and only wreak havoc occasionally
until in time
long as it may be
you get beyond trying to figure it out
asking why

Death Scares Me

death scares me

not my own
it is the death of others
that brings me to my knees
makes me wince and cower in fear
makes me hide from the trembling bodies
makes me run
from seeing faces contorted in pain
the faces of those who loved
and were left behind, abandoned

I want to be far away
to disappear
unable to carry the weight of tears
the suffering and torment I can still feel
and know they feel
I want to be excused for my weakness
forgiven for my cowardice

death scares me

The Eyes in the Mirror

the eyes staring back at me
from the mirror
are not mine
they belong to a stranger
weeping like a caged song
limping along with a cane
bent over at the waist
by the weight of tears
that forces his head to the ground
lost in the impossibility of change
paralyzed by his attachment to insecurity
offered up as rapture and salvation
repeated in his brain over and over again
lying to himself atop a swamp
of rotting silence and mystifying surprise
where the unfortunate waste away
in disillusionment
especially about the power of hope
where he arrives too late to cry
and too young to understand

the eyes staring back at me
from the mirror
are not mine
they belong to a stranger
running down the dark side of the moon
from crumbling rainbows
his wrinkled flesh
hangs loosely from ancient arms
refusing to carry anything more
tired of war and work
our fever-crushed planet
and all that stays the same
swimming against the rising morning tide
he is swept on to the hot sand

to languish in the sun
amidst the debris of stagnant dreams
where the helpless linger in cynicism proven right
especially about the loneliness of time
where he is too late to live
and too young to die

Don't Be Surprised, It's Not Me

in the winter of my foolishness
when I am partially bald
and the rest is gray
when I arise stiff and creaking
to pull myself off the sofa
or out of bed
when my hearing asks, "what did you say?"
over and over again
and my memory can't hold the answer for very long
when my eyesight strains to see beyond my nose
and driving at night is a chilling adventure
when my breath smells musty
even after I've brushed my teeth
and my farts stink far worse
don't be surprised if I say
I'm okay, everything's fine
don't be surprised if I tell you not to worry
I never felt better
we'll both know
it's not really me any longer

Sadness

on my way
through the vulnerable sands of time
and past lives
I met a dangerous stranger
a remarkable faker
a charlatan
a magician
a prisoner and guard
of the masters
and social engineers

on my way
through the vulnerable sands of time
and past lives
I met a dangerous stranger
hung upside down, blood rushing to his head
bound and gagged
by a dense cynicism of his own creation
dying and unfree

on my way
through the vulnerable sands of time
and past lives
I met a dangerous stranger
holding only distant memories
of resistance and rebellion
now held captive
in the ordinary
in the same-old-same-old
in the taken-for-granted
in the way-it-is
in the bowels of the status quo

Keeping Safe and Dying

1.

running after blue skies
where it's warm
and the sun likes to shine
I refuse to see what I'm really chasing
excusing my complacency and inaction
content to watch the news
bemoaning the headlines
a spectator to disaster and tragedy
distracting myself
with the play things and chores of the day-to-day
avoiding introspection
easier to fantasize and complain
keeping safe, doing nothing

2.

I climbed the mountain of my promises
flirting fleetingly
with the summer breeze
and the taste of wildflowers
a delightful delicacy on my lips
dripping like sweet nectar
down the cleft of my chin

I thought I would stay there forever
poet
rebel
warrior
never to be turned around
or sent away
how little I knew then
about the pressure to conform
to join, to be the same
to belong
so now I live on my knees
even though I know
it's killing me

To Be Lonely

to find yourself in a place
where your life is of no value
where your life is worthless
where you don't matter to anyone
is to know what it means
to be lonely

In Death

in death
my life hovers with rage
looking down upon the unfulfilled promises
I knew I would not keep
but promised anyway
and lived with them
like a wart that refused to heal
tormenting myself
even now
as I take my last breath

Once I Was

once I was a dancer
a rock 'n' roll star
a filmmaker
a famous writer
a wise leader
the center of attention
of gravity
of affection...
...once I walked on dreams

Just Me at the Door

never was the poet I hoped to be
or wrote a great novel
never played the piano or the drums
or sang lead in a rock 'n' roll band
never directed a movie
or saw myself on the big screen
never heard the applause of the crowd
or was recognized on the street
never learned to be humble
or how to let go of my ego
it's just me
all I've not become
knocking on the door
to the next time

After I'm Gone

after I'm gone
I hope those who love you
hear the music
I've asked to have played
soaring in all your hearts
and that you sing together
with laughter cascading
like a waterfall
as I am singing now

after I'm gone
I hope those who love you
hold each other close
in tender embrace
and dance
with tears of joy
streaming everywhere
as I am free now

At My Funeral

at my funeral
I'll dance and laugh with you
and with Micah and Jesse too
I'll hold you close
and kiss your lips
one more time
hug you goodbye
one more time
dancing and laughing

Lies and Unfinished Truths

where did they go
the soothing shade trees of my youth
the dreams I thought could be real
the memories I seem to recall
blown away by a blue moon
they collapse into the abyss of fantasy
where I once dwelled very comfortably
clearly
distinctly
imaginatively
now transformed into foggy images
of lies and half-truths
and what might have been
my life of wishful thinking
wanting so badly to be genuine
to be what I had hoped
that's what I fear most about death
knowing the lies and unfinished truths
I'll carry into the darkness
and the light of my next life

Transformation

you are allowed to fly
in the flames of a funeral pyre
permission is granted
to let your spirit consume itself
and be reborn
you are freed
to celebrate death and birth
your soon-to-be-forgotten story
recorded in the book of ages
joining all the stories
of souls like yours
that have passed this way before
and then disappeared
only to be remembered in the fog of past lives
that sit talking with you on a summer's night
sipping iced tea
and gazing through the clouds ringing the moon
reminder of the great circle
matter to energy
and back again
earth to heaven to earth
constantly
always
each passage
unique like a snowflake
forming and melting at the same time

Friends Forever

the past was once a stranger
unknown to the present
but now they are friends forever
seamless contemporaries
who walk hand in hand
hard to tell them apart
where one starts or ends
each day becoming more alike
twins
clones
transforming into the future
with only a change of their clothes

Parking for the (Imagined) Privileged

the signs say:
busses only
small cars only
service vehicles only
handicapped parking
pedestrian crosswalk
do not block driveway
no standing
no parking anytime

the imagined privileged pay no attention
rich, poor, and in-between
they never mind the signs
it's their manifest destiny
to park wherever they like

Cancer of the Mouth

warning signs - if you experience:
spouting hyperbole
a forked tongue
speaking from both sides of your mouth
interrupting
raising your voice
talking in abbreviations
gossiping
spreading rumors
practicing double-speak or
telling bold-faced lies
see your doctor immediately
as these may be signs
of cancer of the mouth

Cowboys and Churches

blond-haired, virgin cowgirls adorned in white hats
riding fast atop pounding hooves
matching the virility and bravado of bucking broncos
with quiet confidence
the sound of sweet purity
blanketing the tobacco-chewing, spur-cutting, chaps-wearing
black-dirt rodeo floor
a thick mix of aromas
of culture and concessions
they pray in their stadium churches for prosperity
more than just the sale of popcorn and hotdogs
sugar loaded sodas and beer
here there is a cross to bear
for Him
intolerant of gays and condoms
but fine with gunslingers and confederate flags
and misogyny with a smile
while clowns divert the bull's attention
just in time to spew anti-gay slurs
in the narrative of western bumper stickers
glued to pick-ups and four wheelers
a foot-stomping spectacle
of the anthem
in whose tribute we honor veterans
roping them like calves on the run
their hind legs bound tight
wrapped all around by the pungent smell
of manure

Road Warrior

his young sun-cracked face
half shaven and roughly hewn
turns in slow motion
toward the car in front of me
"slow down," he waves
walkie-talkie and ponytail
swinging with mild fury
through the acrid smell of hot tar
but it's too late
the driver ahead has already passed by
oblivious
eyes glued to the narrow broken road
and the bright orange pylons separating safety from danger

and then it is my turn
I crawl by nodding a greeting
shrugging my shoulders in acknowledgement
"what the fuck," I say without a word
he smiles slightly
appreciative of the notice and shared understanding
the short-lived respite
from the boredom of stop-to-slow endless swiveling
as he ushers me on my way

Waitress

young, pretty prairie girl
your sleek black dress
lifting your breasts
as you bend to serve milkshakes and fries
burgers and homemade pie-a-la-mode
and always wearing a smile

easy-going single mom
homegrown girl
working the day shift
back and forth on your feet
nurturing locals and tourists
until the clock strikes 5:00
and when you get home
a clinging two year old wherever you go
wanting this, crying for that
tucked into bed with a goodnight kiss
and then finally a moment to rest
watch the news
fall asleep
the next thing you know
its another year

waitress, waitress
so alluring in your western refrain
your walk and the way
you hold your hand on your hip
bringing breakfast all day
chicken and fried steak
Bison stew and cold beer
to satisfy hungry men
unabashed to look you up and down
for the thousandth time
thinking about what they want for dessert
and you
glad that they still do

Inglorious

she wears life on her face
hard and rough lines
etched deeply
shadow filled furrows
distinct in their beaten down stare
nineteen going on ninety
she walks with a stoop
hunched over, head down
preoccupied with the weight

preoccupied with the weight
a Coke can in one hand
a child in tow
her cell phone tight between
her shoulder and ear
swish, she crosses the street in a blur
harried as always
resigned
never enough time

never enough time
to get everything done
the laundry
the cleaning
the shopping
the cooking
the doctor
the dentist
the car repair
the bills
the dropping off
the picking up
the job
the trash and recycling
the inglorious side
of being a single mom

Living and Dying Hard
(a requiem for Margaret Sanchez)

1.

Margaret was one of those people
I didn't see
she lived pretty close to us
but she was invisible to me
until one year
when she taught "Arts," part-time
where our children went to elementary school
"Margaret Day" they called it
for which they had to wear
their "Margaret Day shoes"
not long after
we asked her to tutor one of our boys
so once a week
Margaret came to our home

I saw she had three children of her own
Asian, adopted
that she was a single mom
struggling to survive
I saw her house when I drove by
a small, rumble-tumble kind of place
needing repair and a coat of paint
I saw the newspaper she delivered
before the start of the school day
every morning at 5:00 a.m.
I saw her holding down a job at the bakery
all at the same time
trying to make ends meet
which never did

I saw when her car was parked in her driveway
when she was away and when she was home
and learned toward the end of that year
that Margaret spent many dark hours
fighting weariness and despair
battling to muster up her strength
soothing her body and heart any way she could
drugs and alcohol to help her cope
it may have been part of the reason
she was overlooked for a full-time teaching position
rejected, devalued, and hurt
so much pain and desperateness
and too much to drink
until finally Margaret burst out
loudly jabbering away at graduation
a sad and poignant display
of anger and hopelessness

2.

our boys asked me why Margaret killed herself
I told them
she lived too hard
and was uncared for
she got lost
and couldn't find her way home
she became cold inside
and turned ill
her soul let go
so she could start again

Adolescence

in the anonymity of heads-down adolescent alienation
entrusted to street-smart social engineers
relationships are lost in the fog of days
cut-off by labels and class
opaque windows and shadows
that protect from the glare of openness
of contact
of what might be discovered
if only they could see

but on eyes-up, I know-you days
when they play music and Ultimate Frisbee
drive too fast
and meet under moonlight
even sunglasses and headphones
don't deter at least a wave and smile "hello"
acknowledgement that they belong to each other
and understand the strength of being together

Graciousness and Triumph
(for Jamal)

in the moment of stolen glory and heartbreak
where the greatest efforts
are vanquished by plain bad luck
where an inbounds pass
goes suddenly and surprisingly astray
and missed opportunity ticks loudly away
becoming a "hail Mary" extra three points
for the other side
courage and humility
win huge
all of our spirits triumph
and cannot ever be lost
or taken away
by the illusion of defeat

Rick
(July 1992)

I'm not sure how I will remember him
only that surely I will
perhaps as a laughing dolphin
bounding through the water
outward going and playful like the wind
friendly and wearing a contented smile
perhaps as a soaring eagle
gliding on the sky
quick-witted and swift as lightning
tenacious and always with a keen eye

I'm not sure how I will remember him
only that surely I will
perhaps as a kayak thin yet sturdy
cutting across the swells of Queen Charlotte Sound
graceful and quiet like the deer on shore
smooth-skinned and tan
perhaps as the sleek Orca
diving beneath the sea
powerful and confident
swimming ever onward, proud and free
perhaps as a Mamaleeqala warrior
brave and undaunted
giving unselfishly
devoted to family and tribe

I'm not sure how I will remember him
only that surely I will
perhaps as a loyal St. Bernard
coming to the rescue
steadfast and reliable
no matter what the obstacles
perhaps as a soothsayer
offering an open heart
faithful and loving
to anyone in need

I'm not sure how I will remember him
only that surely I will
perhaps as the person he is
filled with rugged bravado
chauvinistic in a chivalrous fashion
a rags to riches "real lady's man"
perhaps as the human being in which he believes
honest and genuine
cooperative and kind
always willing to lend a hand
perhaps as someone undeterred by torment and pain
possessing the depth of character
to take the good with the bad
the laughter and the hurt
of being so very alive

Reclaimed: The Sacred Journey Poems

Part I: Colorado River Journal
July-August 1990

Put-In

blazing hot, sun baked cliffs
swallow up the tiny passengers
the Dorie glides lazily down river
a brilliant cloudless sky
shines upon the ice-cold Colorado
scarlet, red, and pink
dresses the rock sculptures
they watch silently
while riffles turn to rapids
singing the canyon song
rising to the evening lullaby
sleeping bags laid open upon the sand
shooting stars
and the Milky Way

Morning to Afternoon to Morning

1.

early morning shadows
break across the pristine beach
the sun stretches and yawns
slowly climbing down the layered cliffs
neatly placed in primordial order
a warm Santayana wind
swirls playfully around castles of rock
an eagle and a raven compete for air-space
scavenging the murky red, iron-colored water
and the touches of green, spattered beyond
a brood of baby ducks
scurry for the shore
close behind their mother

2.

nudged down river by a waterfall
spraying mist upon the ruins of ancient cities
citadels of the past
remnants of a wiser civilization
preserved in prehistoric time
stretching upward to meet the late afternoon sky
that soon turns lavender and purple
with night thunder
and rain
and just as quickly
becomes morning cobalt sky
perfect blue

Campsite

bats, red ants, and snakes,
lizards and ravens
creatures of all kinds and sizes
going their own way
abiding by their routines and rituals
as do we
leaving each other undisturbed
uninterrupted
we extend every courtesy
well aware that we are in their home
wanting to be seen
as unexpected visitors
rather than as invaders

Rapid

we paddle through cold wet crests
that spray a refreshing mist
and then suddenly wash over us
cleansed and baptized
plunged into a deep hole

and then reborn
testimony to this spiritual journey
that calls up my oneness and insignificance
I join the flow of the river
a drop in the universe
where I travel now

Time

majestic motley-colored time
pink and tan time
green and brown time
shadowy, sun-bright time
hazy, crisp time
lush, barren time
gentle, strong time
silent, thunderous time
past, present time
non-existent time
all time

Emergence

I rest on the rim
legs straddling a human-made, stone wall
on one side, the canyon sinks sharply away
on the other
roads, storefronts, and restaurants abound
out-of-place in space and time
a passerby chatters about a TV ad
another sniffs the air with disdain
unwelcoming of the fragrant aroma
of mule dung
wafting up from Bright Angel trail
from which I've come
cameras click like a million clocks
golf pants and Bermuda shorts adorn
the sounds of cars and busses and bustle
the language of a strange tongue
a civilization far removed
from the quiet heartbeat of life

Part II: Hawaii Honeymoon Journal Reprise
October-November 1997

Maui

Volcano

1.

we stand at the cold iron railing
bodies shivering, teeth chattering
sipping coffee to warm our hands
they shake nonetheless
nervously we wait to descend
into the ambiguous

2.

swirls of dark gray mist
separate us from the volcano floor
and the sun soon to be rising
we wait patiently for her majesty
gradually the light lifts her head
slowly revealing the contours below
charcoal grays and blacks
touches of red and brown
sloping upwards
grasping for the clouds
illuminating the valley
stretching into wakefulness
vibrant pinks and purples
the rushing blood of morning
filling the sky
her majesty stares us in the eye
we bow in reverence
humbled by her regal crown of red and gold
sighing at the knowledge of how small we are
a tiny blip in time

3.

when we begin downhill the pavement is dry
we glide down easily and exhilarated
but soon we're wiping the clouds from our glasses
getting wet and feeling a bit cold
building up speed on the slick road
testing our brakes
keeping our composure
still in control
we go cycling
a dozen of us
one close behind the other
like ducklings following their mother
racing through lush landscape
tropical dreams and an earlier time
pineapple and sugar cane
beautiful homes and sharecropper shacks
vast, dramatic mountains growing taller
as we approach the crater floor

Panhandling

where wealth and plenty abound
the art of panhandling
is practiced by bell-hops
valet parking attendants
and transplanted valley girls serving drinks
their uniforms
only slightly covering their outstretched hands
like the emperor in his new clothes
they believe they can't be seen begging

Road to Hana

1.

over and over again we've been told
"Hana is about twenty-one miles away
very slow-going,
figure four hours round-trip,
longer if you stop"

over and over again we've been told
"the road to Hana is pretty narrow,
there are thirty-four twists and turns,
and seven one-lane bridges,
don't forget to honk your horn
and flash your brights"

2.

we start early, optimistically
convertible top down
confident we'll enjoy clear weather
on the heels of last night's storm
through which we cuddled and swooned
the warmth of our bodies soothing our wary hearts
but after only several miles
the blue-gray sky pours tears
making the winding switchbacks to Hana
a bit more challenging
like our lives now
twisting and turning in sadness and uncertainty
our own tears splash up from the road
distance settles in
like a thick, cold cloud
we ride politely
amiably, amicably
I hardly know you

Even the Falls of Wiamu

1.

small stretches of open land and wide paths
looked after by mountain stewards
turn into a narrow smile
lined by thick underbrush
and stands of richly matted bamboo
a canopy of Guavas heavy with fruit
hangs precariously overhead
not far away, a Banyan tree
petrified, prehistoric octopus of the earth
her tentacles reaching for the green-topped ceiling
something makes me think of tigers

2.

we cross a bridge spanning a deep gorge
and walk on wooden footpaths
and neatly placed stones
hesitant, tenuous
not because of our surroundings
but each other
our attempts at closeness
like groping in the dark
"who are you," I wonder
that even the falls of Wiamu do not soothe
"who are you?"
that these soft drops of perfume
falling endlessly
do not heal
"who are you?"

3.

we sit by a clear pool
resting
soaking in the paradise around us
you touch my back
but I am numb, shut down
trying to avoid my reflection in your eyes
protect myself from anguish and pain
cloaked in an unfeeling shell
warding off the fears
that I worry are all too real

4.

we return in silence
nothing to say or share
frozen on the edge
staring blankly
as we view the needle of Iao Valley
in the harsh rain

Kauai

Luxury

1.

we land in Kauai, a bit shaky from the rough flight
we are still trying
still losing

2.

and then
we erupt
as if filled with the molten rock
upon which these islands were created
as if we were part of that rock
part volcano
seething
needing release
leading us to the warmth of a hot bath
and cool champagne
and love-making
the passion we reclaim
a luxury

Last Evening

we sit close together on a cushiony pink sofa
swallowed in its softness
your head resting upon my shoulder
I play with your hair
feeling so small in the rapture of the moment
like a fledgling secure in its nest

a woman's melodic voice
lifts upward to the tranquil blue ceiling
and we, higher still
joined by the notes of a piano
we are lost in the echo
discovered
in the song of birds of paradise
perched on our laps
bringing harmony

Revered Places

1.

even after all these weeks
the fine red dust of the Valley of Fire
clings to the soles of my sandals
holding on to ancient messages
carefully etched into the black-streaked face of time
protected memories of the elements, animals, and people
that left their mark here
and were not to be forgotten or unknown
by those like me
who would find their way through this hallowed ground
imagining what it might have been like
when a Piute on the run rested in the shade
and was sheltered from the blazing sun
finding strength in the flash-flood overhangs and small amphitheaters
randomly carved into a sanctuary of immortal rock

2.

as night beckons daytime to bed
we climb higher
heading toward Bryce
the cool crisp air surprises me
reminiscent of our fall evenings in Vermont
at 8,000 feet my breath is thin
yet thick at the same time
filled with thousands of stars
buffeting the blue velvet sky
invisible mountains sleep soundly
as do we
when we finally close our eyes
to dream of tomorrow's adventure

3.

morning takes us on Navaho Loop
past strangely named formations
"Queen's Garden" and "Wall Street"
so out of touch with the spirit of natural architecture
that leads to Sunrise Point
hoodoos, like sculptured sand castle spires
drip upward
a grand cathedral stretching endlessly
casting a magic spell all around me
I listen carefully for the sound of prayer
and hear my heartbeat
roaming the steep cliffs
as it moves in cadence with coyote ghosts
that the Piute tell
were turned to stone for all eternity

the next day we hike up and down simultaneously
winding our way toward Tower Bridge
expecting to come to a place
where we can cross through the sky
high above the horizon
only to find ourselves sitting on fallen trees
munching fruit and nuts in a small clearing
looking up I see the wonder we were seeking
that we thought would offer passage to the other side
inaccessible to the likes of me

I am not disappointed
the hike back satisfies my need for exercise
and for sacred views of the world
they wash into my sleep
alive with images of comforting beauty
and the sounds of a peaceful quiet
in which I can rest

4.

the sun rises with gentle anticipation
Anasazi ancestors murmur in the wind
sweetly whispering in my ear "Mukuntuweap"
renamed "Zion" by Mormon pioneers
that in Hebrew means "refuge"
which clearly it is
and so much more
a transcendent haven
where the pure, life-blood waters of the Virgin River
give sustenance to hanging gardens and canyon tree frogs
to black chinned hummingbirds
and emerald pools nesting in clouds
where spirit and religion are inspired by nature's soul
from which there rises a call for stewardship
the mutual honoring of revered places
given names like "Altar of Sacrifice" and "Angels Landing"
the "Court of the Patriarchs" and
the "Temple of Sinawava"

Our House Would Be Too Quiet
(to Micah)

our house would be too quiet
without the music of your piano
filling our ears
our hearts empty and bleak
without your brave melodies
waves crashing against steep cliffs
drama unfolding in every chord

our house would be too quiet
without your hands caressing the keys
discovering your soul's delight
our days so lonely
without your highs and lows
the courage you own
leaving its mark on every note

our house would be too quiet
without the sound of your drums
keeping a steady beat
our relationship left incomplete
without the base resounding
the walls between us vibrating and shaking
coming down all around

our house would be too quiet
without the pounding of your cymbals
giving life to your passions
our time sadly unfulfilled
without the stamina you show
playing to your own truths
and an audience that loves you

To Tell the Truth
(Reprise)

in the telling of the truth
that finds its way through darkness and light
and the gift of mystery
my story is written
as it really was
and might have been
thin threads woven of sadness and exhilaration
moments when nothing remained the same
and by the telling, by the writing
are transformed again

in the telling of the truth
that traces its way upon paths taken
memory blunted by time
my story is written
as it really was
and might have been
thin threads woven of reality and fantasy
moments when I was changed
and by the telling, by the writing
I am changed again

About the Author

Ron grew up in the ocean side neighborhood of Belle Harbor in Queens, New York. As a sophomore at Brooklyn College (1967) he became deeply involved in social-political activism. After graduating from college and a brief stint at American University Law School Ron returned to Brooklyn, NY where from 1970-1974 he lived, taught elementary school, attended graduate school, and continued his activism. Ron moved to Vermont during the summer of 1974 and has lived in the college town of Middlebury for the past twenty-nine years. He shares his life and writing with his wife, Lisa, their two boys, Micah and Jesse, and their precious community of friends.

Adaptive Tensions is Ron's sixteenth book of poetry. He gives all of his books away for free or on occasion, sells them at cost. This is his small way of sharing his gifts and strengths; walking his talk; and being open hearted to his world.

www.ingramcontent.com/pod-product-compliance
Lightning Source LLC
Chambersburg PA
CBHW020616300426
44113CB00007B/669
* 9 7 8 0 9 9 6 5 8 4 9 0 6 *